Heaven Is for Real

Heaven Is for Real

A Little Boy's Astounding Story of His Trip to Heaven and Back

CONVERSATION GUIDE™

Todd Burpo

THOMAS NELSON
Since 1798

NASHVILLE   DALLAS   MEXICO CITY   RIO DE JANEIRO

Published in Nashville, Tennessee, by Thomas Nelson. Thomas Nelson is a trademark of Thomas Nelson, Inc.

The publisher would like to extend thanks to Phil Harris for his assistance in preparing this manuscript. The publisher would also like to thank Dawn Sherill and Brenda Noel of ECHO Creative Media for their collaboration in developing the content for this guide.

Author is represented by the literary agency of Alive Communications.

Thomas Nelson, Inc., titles may be purchased in bulk for educational, business, fund-raising, or sales promotional use. For information, please e-mail SpecialMarkets@ThomasNelson.com.

Unless otherwise indicated, Scripture quotations are taken from the Holy Bible, New International Version®, NIV®. Copyright © 1973, 1978, 1984 by Biblica, Inc.™ Used by permission of Zondervan. All rights reserved worldwide. www .zondervan.com

Scripture quotations marked NKJV are taken from THE NEW KING JAMES VERSION. © 1982 by Thomas Nelson, Inc. Used by permission. All rights reserved.

978-1-4185-50684-001

Printed in the United States of America

11 12 13 14 15 16 QG 6 5 4 3 2 1

Contents

Introduction

Get up early. Take care of the kids. Go to work. Find something
for dinner. Get ready for tomorrow. This is real life; and we
know all about real life, as we face it and its trials with each new
day. We know the face of death, too: cancer, heart attacks, car
accidents, illness—it's all too real.

But what happens after that final earthly breath? How can
we know what waits on the other side? What does our existence
look like in the world beyond the only one we know?

Death is a mystery for all. For those who don't know Jesus,
the thought of death can be terrifying. Christians around the
world know we have the eternal home of heaven waiting for us.
But death remains mysterious, and the unknown can bring fear
in its wake, even for those whose faith in Jesus Christ gives them
assurance of life after death.

Through *Heaven Is for Real*, you shared Colton's miraculous
glimpse of the world that awaits us when our time on this earth
is done. This study guide will lead you, together with your small
group, on an even more dynamic and candid journey with our
family—a journey that will allow you to experience through
Colton's eyes and apprehend through God's Word the truth
regarding eternity and what it holds for those who know Jesus.

Colton chose the name for his book; he wants everyone to know that heaven is definitely "for real." He wants all to discover the truth in Jesus' words, "For God so loved the world that He gave His only begotten Son, that whoever believes in Him should not perish but have everlasting life. For God did not send His Son into the world to condemn the world, but that the world through Him might be saved. He who believes in Him is not condemned; but he who does not believe is condemned already, because he has not believed in the name of the only begotten Son of God" (John 3:16–18 NKJV).

For those who do not know Jesus as their Savior, this study will act as a guide to Jesus—the Way, the Truth, and the Life—and will help you learn how you can experience the kingdom of God both today and eternally. For Christians, this guide is a call to share what we know is true, to put uncertainty behind us, and to let others know and rest assured that heaven is a real place that awaits those who have made Jesus Christ their Savior and Lord.

The *Heaven Is for Real* Group Experience

This study is based on Colton's story and our family's experiences since we shared Colton's tour of heaven with the world. Its purpose is to strengthen those who already know the

Lord and to enlighten those who do not. We will discuss many aspects of our family's experience, going to the Word of God as the final authority. We hope you find the time you spend exploring the biblical foundations of *Heaven Is for Real* with your small group to be encouraging, challenging, and life changing.

Your small group is an expression of the body of Christ in action. Each member has a unique view and a necessary voice. To encourage candid and open participation in this group, we want to create an environment in which everyone is valued equally, regardless of his or her spiritual faith definition; and where all are encouraged share freely, question, and comment without fear or hesitation. All are encouraged to be authentic and transparent and to participate to the degree that they are able. To this end, we need to realize that compassion and respect are key elements of small group life. These are lived out through listening to one another, praying for and encouraging one another, and holding in strict confidence anything of a personal nature shared within your group. Criticizing or condemning one another will only serve to discourage sharing and limit your small group experience.

Remember, as with most things in life, you will get as much from this study as you are willing to give. Approach it with an open mind. Set aside the time with your small group to grow closer to the Lord and receive from His Spirit. Take time throughout the week to read God's Word and discover for yourself the revelations regarding the abundant life available in God's kingdom today and His eternal promises for the world to come. Pray diligently for the people in your small group, and celebrate together as you watch the Holy Spirit "shoot down power" to transform circumstances, change hearts, and heal lives.

Now let's join our hearts and minds together as we learn more about eternity and how to walk in powerful, childlike, confident faith.

How to Use This Guide

The reaction to Colton's story as told in *Heaven Is for Real* has been extraordinary. For some the book has been a tremendous encouragement and source of healing; for others, it has been a source of confusion and animosity. We felt strongly that we should address those concerns as well as provide greater insight into our experiences and the biblical foundations of our message. *Heaven Is for Real* is the story; this study will take you beyond the story into the kingdom dynamics and biblical truth surrounding Colton's experiences in heaven and our family's experiences since our story became known.

DVD

During your small group time, you will watch a DVD together that will address different aspects of Colton's experience and the issues that have arisen since his time in heaven. Each DVD session is divided into two sections: an introductory message and an interview with Colton and our family. Although it is not necessary to read *Heaven Is for Real* before you walk with us through this study, we strongly encourage you to read it first in order to better relate to the events discussed in the video.

DISCUSSION

So many questions exist in all our minds regarding death. You may simply want to face this issue in light of biblical truth; maybe you find the reality of your own death to be a fearful one; or possibly the death of a loved one has left you with a broken heart or empty arms. Regardless of the reason you chose to begin this journey, your small group can be a source of support and encouragement.

We chose to format this study for a small group in order to provide an atmosphere of community—a "mini body of Christ," so to speak. As the apostle Paul said, "For as we have many members in one body, but all the members do not have the same function, so we, being many, are one body in Christ, and individually members of one another" (Romans 12:4–5 NKJV).

Your group is made up of people who desire to know more about the Lord and His kingdom. It is a safe place to share your questions, concerns, sorrows, and pain. As you share openly and allow others to explore their own thoughts and feelings as you discover truth together, all will be strengthened.

For each session of this study, we have provided discussion questions or topics to enhance your experience. These should be considered discussion starters, not a road map. Don't be concerned if all the questions for each session are not addressed. The important thing in this study is real, authentic, open, and honest sharing. When seekers and believers operate in love, compassion, and honesty, the power of the Holy Spirit will lead all to the truth. Dare to be transparent; take a chance on your group, and be a willing vessel of love and compassion. You will find the reward is well worth the risk.

REAL REFLECTIONS

After each session, you will find a personal devotion section titled "Real Reflection." This portion of the guide is designed to help you dig deeper into God's Word and further develop your relationship with our Lord. You will be presented with further Scripture reading and devotional or inspirational topics to encourage and solidify your faith. Personal time with the Lord is critical to a life of faith. We strongly encourage you to set aside time each day to talk to God, read His Word, and bask in the love that flows from Him toward you. As Colton says, "He really, really loves us . . . You can't *belieeeve* how much he loves us!"

JOURNAL

During our time together, we will examine many issues that will touch our lives and impact our hearts deeply. We will spend quality time together each week; but hopefully, we will each spend some very intimate, quality time thinking about our time together and prayerfully asking Jesus to give us understanding and faith. Whenever we take time to truly consider the truth of God's Word, Jesus will speak to our hearts and minds. Although space has been provided in this guide to record your thoughts, you may find a notebook to be valuable, especially as you spend time with the Lord during your Real Reflections each week. You will not be required to share what you write in your journal, though you may if you choose. So you can feel totally free to write out your questions, put your feelings into words, and record the truth you discover as you seek the Lord and listen for His voice.

BRINGING IT HOME

As you walk through this time with your small group, the insights you gain will be life changing. You may wish to share your experience with your family. In order to equip you to include your family in your journey, we have included family discussion topics and questions at the end of each session. You can tailor these suggestions to fit your own family dynamics and personality.

Our family has experienced together the encouragement and hope generated by Colton's trip to heaven. It is our desire that you and your family experience the wonder, peace, and lifelong hope in knowing that *heaven is for real.*

Why Should We Care About Heaven?

Colton knows for certain that heaven is for real, and so do we. We are an ordinary family in the midst of extraordinary circumstances, desiring to be faithful to God and to be a source of encouragement to those who encounter us and our story. The message of the reality of heaven we've been given to share is serious and powerful because it deals with eternal truth. It is a message of hope and peace. The world is full of seekers desperately trying to find truth, hope, and peace. God can use Colton's journey to speak directly to those needs. We pray that the clarity of his four-year-old's description of our eternal home can cut through the confusions of this world, wherever they are found, even in the minds and spirits of those who are already believers in Jesus Christ.

We have discovered that our family is not alone. All over the body of Christ, we have found people who identify with our experiences and who are encouraging one another and building one another up in the faith (see 1 Thessalonians 5:11).

But whenever a message is shared, there will always be skeptics. In view of the importance of this message, careful, open-minded consideration is wise. Some people are determined not to believe, no matter what the evidence. It's not for us to argue and convince. It is for us to share this reality as faithfully as we can, just as it is every Christian's job to share the realities of Christ and our eternal home. We pray that our journey will be a strong witness to those who don't believe, but also be a strengthening balm to those who do.

We have seen the power of the Word of God in our lives. Colton's experience has only strengthened our faith in God's Word and its unalterable truth. It is powerful and relevant to our lives today, and for eternity. So now we want to spend time in Scripture, our final authority, to explore why we should care about heaven.

Group Discussion

 Why did you decide to participate in this study?

Is the reality of heaven something you have ever thought or cared about before today? Why or why not?

Do you believe we will experience an afterlife? If so, what concepts of heaven or of afterlife have you previously held?

Watch Session 1 Intro Video Message

Who is God? That is a question we must be able to answer for ourselves. In order to pray in true, believing power, we must know the One whose touch we seek. To share our faith in Christ with others, we must be able to introduce them to our Father.

The one true God, the God Colton met in heaven, is the holy Trinity: God the Father, God the Son (Jesus), and God the Holy Spirit (Genesis 1:2–3; 2 Samuel 23:2–3; Job 33:4; Micah 5:2; John 1:1–3, 14; 8:58, 10:30; 15:26). He is real and personal and holy. So when we say, "God," we are not referring to a generic "higher power," or a god we've made up from our own wishes, but the holy God of heaven and earth, the Author of eternity.

It is a fact that God, in some form, however mistaken, is acknowledged by most; however, far too often, Jesus is invisible. The One who revealed to us the very character and nature of God (John 14:8–10), the One who died so that we could know the Father and live eternally with Him (John 17:3), is conspicuously absent from most aspects of society.

Group Discussion

What thoughts do you have when you consider the nature of God as Father, Son, and Holy Spirit? Can you think of examples in God's Word, the Bible, that would enable you to better grasp this difficult concept?

✺ Have you noticed the absence of Jesus, even in places where God may be acknowledged? Does that trouble you? Why or why not?

✺ What are some examples of "gods" we try to create for ourselves? How do they stand up against the one true God we find in Scripture?

✺ Being totally honest, describe God's nature or value in your own experience.

✸ How important is it to be clear on God's identity?

Watch DVD Session 1

Just as it is important to know what we mean by "God," it's
vital to know what we mean by "heaven." We are not talking
about a hybrid destination that some religions call "nirvana,"
"becoming one with the universe," or "reincarnation" of some
form or other. We are talking about the eternal home prepared
by God for those who have believed in and followed Him, a
home made available to us through the salvation provided by
Jesus Christ, His Son. We're talking about everlasting closeness
to God in the place where He has righted all wrongs and healed
all wounds of this present world. Heaven is the fulfillment of
God's kingdom and our life in Him.

Knowing the reality of this eternal home can be the life
preserver that keeps our heads above water when life becomes
overwhelming. Holding a biblically valid perspective can help us
keep walking, even when the problems of the world challenge

every step. We will spend eternity somewhere, so it is vital to
think about, and know to our fullest ability, where that will be.
In Colton's words, it is so important to know that "heaven is for
real."

Scripture

- John 5:24–29:

  "Most assuredly, I say to you, he who hears My word and
  believes in Him who sent Me has everlasting life, and shall
  not come into judgment, but has passed from death into life.
  Most assuredly, I say to you, the hour is coming, and now
  is, when the dead will hear the voice of the Son of God; and
  those who hear will live. For as the Father has life in Himself,
  so He has granted the Son to have life in Himself, and has
  given Him authority to execute judgment also, because He is
  the Son of Man. Do not marvel at this; for the hour is coming
  in which all who are in the graves will hear His voice and
  come forth—those who have done good, to the resurrection
  of life, and those who have done evil, to the resurrection of
  condemnation." (NKJV)

- Matthew 25:32–34, 41, 46:

  "All the nations will be gathered before Him, and He will
  separate them one from another, as a shepherd divides his
  sheep from the goats. And He will set the sheep on His right
  hand, but the goats on the left. Then the King will say to
  those on His right hand, 'Come, you blessed of My Father,
  inherit the kingdom prepared for you from the foundation
  of the world' . . . Then He will also say to those on the left
  hand, 'Depart from Me, you cursed, into the everlasting fire
  prepared for the devil and his angels' . . . And these will go
  away into everlasting punishment, but the righteous into
  eternal life." (NKJV)

- Romans 6:23:

  For the wages of sin is death, but the gift of God is eternal life
  in Christ Jesus our Lord. (NKJV)

Group Discussion

✸ Has what we've discussed in this session changed your view of heaven? If so, how so?

✸ How does your current view of heaven contrast with your prior concepts?

✸ What first intrigued you about Colton's story? What encouraging experiences have you already had or heard about, stemming from the sharing of his journey?

✸ How have you been strengthened to share your faith and your own stories?

✸ John 5:24–29 makes it very clear that we will all spend eternity somewhere—we will either live in eternal life or everlasting condemnation. How can knowing that eternal life, true life with God, is your ultimate future help you face the challenges you have on this earth? How does knowing the reality of unending condemnation for those who do not know Christ motivate you to share the truth of salvation and eternal security in Him?

In Matthew 25, we see this truth shown even further. Heaven is the kingdom created for us "from the foundation of the world" (v. 34 NKJV). God prepared our eternal home before we even came into being. How does that fact affect the way you think about heaven?

In light of John 5 and Matthew 25, why should we care about heaven?

☀ In the beginning of this session, we discussed how society acknowledges God, yet tragically ignores Jesus. What does Romans 6:23 tell us about the presence of God the Father and Jesus when it comes to eternity? Who is the source of our eternal life in heaven?

Prayer

Lord, we thank You for loving us enough to provide salvation from our sins and to prepare an eternal home for us. We pray that You will bless our study and allow Your Word to speak to us, teach us, challenge us, encourage us, and renew us. We thank You for the journey You've given to Colton and his family, and for their faithfulness in sharing it. Please be with us as we continue to encounter the reality of your kingdom.

Real Reflection

It is so difficult for us to even imagine the glorious world Colton visited. How can our limited human minds conceive of the eternal wonders of God?

Colton used the words he knew at the age of four to attempt to describe the incomparable beauty and indescribable majesty of our Father's kingdom. His experience is much like the apostle John's, recorded in the book of Revelation, as John attempted to convey sights and sounds that were beyond his understanding. The apostle knew that mere words could not fully communicate the awesome richness of heaven, so more than sixty times he described his experience using the comparative "like." (See, for example, Revelation 1:10, 13; 4:1, 6–7; 6:1; 8:8, 10.)

But through the eyes of a child, we have been given a glimpse of the sublime experience that awaits those who know the Son of God.

PERSONAL REFLECTION

Read Deuteronomy 4:29 and Matthew 7:7–8.

Seek Him and you will find Him! God is available and ready to meet you when you set your heart on seeking His face.

We may not be able to sit on Jesus' lap and know the feel of His tender touch. We may not be granted the joy of looking into the loving eyes of our Savior before the day He takes us home. It may be the other side of eternity that reveals to us the glory of God's throne. But Jesus tells us we can know Him now. Through prayer and studying His Word, we can have the unparalleled contentment of intimacy with the Lord. Our Savior promises that He will reveal Himself to those who seek Him. Spend time with the Lord. Learn the gentle timbre of His voice as He speaks to your soul. Begin to hear the very heartbeat of your Creator as you encounter the Author of life. Drink deep of the water of life that pours forth for all who come near to God's throne of grace. Experience the joy of looking deep into the eyes of the very Source of life and love—our eternal, triune God: Father, Son, and Holy Spirit.

POINTS TO PONDER

- What does it mean to discover intimacy with Jesus Christ as Lord?

- What steps can you take to make intimacy with Jesus a reality in your life?

- Are prayer and Bible study an important part of your life? How much time do you spend with the Lord each day? Does that amount of time accurately reflect His importance in your life?

- Write down the words that honestly describe your faith relationship with Christ.

  _____

  _____

  _____

- Write down the words that truthfully describe your relationship with His church.

  _____

  _____

  _____

- What is your reaction to the descriptors you've used in the previous two questions? If your relationships with the Lord and His church are not what you desire them to be, how can improve these relationships?

Journal

Bringing It Home

- Why should we care about heaven?

- Read Revelation 21:1–5, 23–27; 22:1–5. What do you learn from these passages?

- Describe how you see heaven.

- Who lives in heaven?

- What do you think it will be like to see Jesus for the first time?

- What do you think it will be like to see God for the first time?

- What are some things that happen to you that make you sad?

- What will it be like to be in a place where you are never sad?

- How do you get to heaven?

Family Prayer

Jesus, we thank You for our family. Thank You for creating a home for us today, and for creating a home for us in heaven that will last forever. Please bless our family, Jesus. Help us always remember how much You love us. Show us how best to love our family, even on days when it seems hard. Help us to know You better every day, and remind us of all the wonderful things You have done for us. Amen.

What Is Heaven Like?

We all have questions about what heaven is like; but trying
to describe heaven is a lot like trying to describe New York
City to someone from an ancient time. Heaven is beyond our
world, outside our dimension. It is a spiritual realm, and we
live in a physical one. We can only use our own limited words,
knowledge, and experiences to communicate things that are
beyond our physical world. Some things Colton saw during his
visit to heaven have been the source of disagreement
and much discussion. We understand that. All we
can do is share what he saw in the best way we
know. But there are certain truths about heaven
that cannot be denied. In this session, we want
to focus on those truths as Colton experienced
them and, most important, as Scripture
describes them.

Jesus said, "In My Father's house are many mansions; if it were not so, I would have told you. I go to prepare a place for you. And if I go and prepare a place for you, I will come again and receive you to Myself; that where I am, there you may be also" (John 14:2–3 NKJV). He also confirmed to us that His Father is our Father (Luke 11:2). What amazing truth: Jesus has prepared a place for us in our heavenly Father's house!

Colton's favorite place in God's house was His throne room. Colton sat there with God the Father, God the Son, and God the Holy Spirit. You may find yourself wishing you could experience that same presence of the one true God. You can! God's throne room is a place where all who believe on the name of Jesus are welcome. God has issued an open invitation to live forever with Him in His house; to accept, we must simply believe in Christ as our personal Savior. Jesus is the door to God's house, giving us entrance into our true home of pure joy, meaning, and purpose.

We can have discussions about particular details of heaven, such as the presence of animals or whether or not we will have wings, but the ultimate truth is that heaven is very real, and we can live there eternally with God.

Now let's go a little further in Colton's journey, exploring the Word of God as we find out even more about what heaven is like.

Group Discussion

❉ What are some specific questions you've had about heaven?

❉ So far in our study, has the idea of heaven become more real to you? Why or why not? If it has become more real to you, in what way?

Watch Session 2
Intro Video Message

When considering what heaven is like, it is often tempting to be overwhelmed by complicated theories or details. Trying to describe an unknown place, much less a heavenly one, can be a massive challenge. We can get caught up in discussions about things such as streets of gold, or whether or not we'll see our pets there. And those aren't bad discussions. But perhaps the essence of what heaven is like doesn't have to be that complex. In the midst of all the details, what is it that truly defines heaven? Very simply, heaven is God's house. God's presence is there, and that is what makes heaven, heaven.

Genesis 1:27 tells us that we are created in God's image. But here on earth, it can be difficult to look in a mirror and see a reflection of the divine. It is easy to get caught up in our shortcomings, failures, and sometimes decidedly ungodly behavior. Yet, we are created in the image of God, and we are the very object of His affection (John 3:16). We were created by Him and for Him, so living eternally in His presence will be our ultimate fulfillment.

Heaven is meant to be our eternal home. As masters of our own homes, we do not grant entry to uninvited, unknown people; they cannot come in and do as they please. We welcome people into our homes who have requested entrance; we open our doors to those we know. We learn through God's Word that Jesus is the door to God's house and the only way into that perfect place (John 10:9). Heaven was prepared for us before the foundation of the world (Matthew 25:34), but entrance into that perfect place will be granted only to those who know heaven's Master, Jesus. None of us can follow our own road to heaven; neither can we map out our own strategies to gain entrance. There is no alternate door.

Jesus told us that He went to prepare a place for those who know Him, and that He will one day return to take them home with Him (John 14:2–3). No sin will be able to break in to God's house; it is not allowed through the door. But even though sin is a fact of all our lives (Romans 3:23), because of Jesus' love and sacrificial death on the cross, our sin is erased and heaven is available to all who will call upon the name of the Lord (Romans 10:13). To be assured of entrance into God's eternal kingdom, to know the perfect joy and peace of heaven, we need only to believe that Jesus is God's Son, that in dying for us He conquered sin, and that in rising from the grave, He conquered death. Through Jesus we can know eternal life in God's presence because Jesus said, "Where I am, there you may be also" (NKJV).

God's house is amazing—a home where no sin, shame, grief, or pain can follow us; an eternal dwelling into which we are all invited; a place where Love Himself rules. If sinful humanity can give and receive love, we can only imagine the love that pours forth from the One who is the very source of love. For you see, God *is* love (1 John 4:7–16), and all are invited to come to know Jesus and be granted entrance into God's timeless kingdom of love.

Group Discussion

✹ Have you previously thought of heaven as God's house? How can this image make heaven seem more personal to you?

✹ Why do you think Jesus chose to use the image of His Father's house to describe heaven?

How does being reminded that you're made in the image of God affect the way you think of yourself? How does it influence the way you see God?

Imagine what it will be like to live without sin and its effects. How will it feel to live without temptation? Without shame? Without the destructive consequences that sin always brings? In the place where Love Himself rules?

Watch DVD Session 2

Colton's experience of heaven was so tangible; it allows us a glimpse of heaven as a real place, and more important, as a real home. We will live there—really, truly *live*, not just exist as misty presences simply floating about in some otherworldly, vaporous place. Often, especially as children, we may imagine heaven to be a place where everyone sits on a cloud and plays a harp for eternity. But neither the Bible nor Colton's experience would have us believe anything of the sort. We will be happily busy in heaven. We will have purpose, meaning, and contentment. We will find ultimate fulfillment in the constant presence of our Father in His house, and experience total peace and joy in all we do . . . for eternity.

To our limited, human intellect, eternity is a nearly mind-boggling concept. God and His eternal kingdom exist outside of infinity, so heaven is a place without time. God is not constrained by the limitations of time and space, as we are. This helps us understand how Colton could have experienced so much in such a short time. On his journey, He visited a place beyond our finite time and space, so our hours, minutes, and seconds didn't apply. Just as the apostle Peter said, "With the Lord, one day is as a thousand years, and a thousand years as one day" (2 Peter 3:8 NKJV). Whether or not you apply that equation mathematically to the three minutes Colton spent on his journey, when you realize that heaven is in no way beholden to our clock, it is much easier to accept that so much happened in such a small segment of earthly time.

While describing details of heaven itself (such as colors, music, animals, or wings) is challenging, relating events outside of time is as well. Colton was able to see events from earthly past, present, and future. While it may be a bit disconcerting to hear your son tell you about a battle you're going to fight in your resurrected body, it is also inspiring to know that one day we will live in a place where time is no longer an enemy, or even an impartial participant, ticking off the moments of our lives.

Colton's visit to heaven has made Scripture become even more vivid and alive to our family; we hope it can do the same for you. We are reminded that we are not simply talking about concepts and stories in the Bible, but about real people and a real, personal God who has prepared a real, personal home for us. So when we see a rainbow, it's not just a beautiful reminder of a Sunday school story. Rather, it is an authentic reminder that we have a genuine God who keeps His promises. When we read in Psalms that we can trust in the shelter of His wings (61:4), we can be assured that we can trust Him completely. When the New Testament talks about having a peace that passes understanding (Philippians 4:7), we know that this is not just pretty language; it is a real peace from Jesus that can sustain us through the most trying of circumstances.

As we have discussed, heaven exists in an infinite realm outside of time and space. We cannot possibly know or comprehend everything about a place so far removed from our earthly experience. But the little we do know can help us realize that the mystery of heaven should excite and encourage us, not frighten or intimidate us. We don't have to look upon the mystery with fear, because we know that beyond it lies even more incredible, beautiful, and indescribable joy than we can imagine.

So let's go to Scripture and see what else we can learn about what heaven is like.

Scripture

- Matthew 13:44–46:

  "Again, the kingdom of heaven is like treasure hidden in a field, which a man found and hid; and for joy over it he goes and sells all that he has and buys that field.

  "Again, the kingdom of heaven is like a merchant seeking beautiful pearls, who, when he had found one pearl of great price, went and sold all that he had and bought it." (NKJV)

- Revelation 7:16–17:

  They shall neither hunger anymore nor thirst anymore; the sun shall not strike them, nor any heat; for the Lamb who is in the midst of the throne will shepherd them and lead them to living fountains of waters. And God will wipe away every tear from their eyes. (NKJV).

- Revelation 21:1–5:

  Now I saw a new heaven and a new earth, for the first heaven and the first earth had passed away. Also there was no more sea. Then I, John, saw the holy city, New Jerusalem, coming down out of heaven from God, prepared as a bride adorned for her husband. And I heard a loud voice from heaven saying, "Behold, the tabernacle of God is with men, and He will dwell with them, and they shall be His people. God Himself will be with them and be their God. And God will wipe away every tear from their eyes; there shall be no more death, nor sorrow, nor crying. There shall be no more pain, for the former things have passed away."

  Then He who sat on the throne said, "Behold, I make all things new." And He said to me, "Write, for these words are true and faithful." (NKJV)

- Revelation 21:10–11:

  And he carried me away in the Spirit to a great and high mountain, and showed me the great city, the holy Jerusalem, descending out of heaven from God, having the glory of God. Her light was like a most precious stone, like a jasper stone, clear as crystal. (NKJV)

- Revelation 21:18–23:

  The construction of its wall was of jasper; and the city was pure gold, like clear glass. The foundations of the wall of the city were adorned with all kinds of precious stones: the first foundation was jasper, the second sapphire, the third chalcedony, the fourth emerald, the fifth sardonyx, the sixth sardius, the seventh chrysolite, the eighth beryl, the ninth topaz, the tenth chrysoprase, the eleventh jacinth, and the twelfth amethyst. The twelve gates were twelve pearls: each individual gate was of one pearl. And the street of the city was pure gold, like transparent glass. But I saw no temple in it, for the Lord God Almighty and the Lamb are its temple. The city had no need of the sun or of the moon to shine in it, for the glory of God illuminated it. The Lamb is its light. (NKJV)

Group Discussion

Jesus often used parables (short, allegorical stories) to describe the kingdom of God. Heaven is the ultimate fulfillment of the kingdom of God, so the parables in Matthew 13 suggest that heaven is a treasure beyond comparing to anything we can have or know on this earth.

❋ What are some of your favorite things that Jesus tells us about heaven? Why are they important to you?

❋ Romans 14:17 tells us that God's kingdom is a place of righteousness, peace, and joy. What experiences come to mind when you consider the word *joy*?

* Describe a time when you felt the most contented and
  peaceful. What insight does that experience give you
  into the "perfect peace" God gives (see Isaiah 26:3 NKJV)?
  How does it encourage you to know that one day you can
  experience that perfect peace eternally?

* Earlier, we discovered that what makes heaven, heaven
  is God's presence. Colton's favorite place in heaven was
  God's throne room. Revelation 21:3 makes it clear that we
  may all one day experience His majestic, loving presence.
  Describe a time when you felt especially close to God.
  How does that experience help you imagine what an
  unhindered, eternal experience of God's presence will be
  like in heaven?

✺ Describe something you have seen in a state of destruction
or decay. What did you think or feel when you saw it?
Has there been a time in your life when you have felt the
crippling effects of devastation or despair? Revelation 21:5
tells us that God will make all things new. Heaven will be
a place of eternal newness, for our surroundings, and
also for us. How does this truth speak into the brokenness
you've encountered in your world or in your own life?

✺ Revelation 21 speaks of the light and city of heaven as
being as clear as crystal and glass (vv. 11, 18). What do you
think is the significance of such clarity and brightness?

✹ According to Revelation 21:23, what is the source of the light in heaven?

✹ What are some areas of your life now that need clarifying by the light of Jesus?

✹ If you had to answer the question, what is heaven like? in your own words, what would you say?

Prayer

Lord, we thank You for providing the way for us to experience Your presence now, and for eternity. Thank you for giving us purpose and peace, even on earth, but especially the perfect peace and everlasting fulfillment waiting for us in heaven. Thank You for the beautiful mystery of our eternal home. Please help us to appreciate all we can know now about Your house and to embrace through faith what we can't yet know. Help us to respond to your Word with the faith and trust that You have prepared incomparable treasures for us out of Your great love. Please continue to lead us in this study, as we seek to know more about You and Your house. Amen.

Real Reflection

When we think about and try to describe what heaven is like, we're often tempted to get bogged down in details or debates. While there's nothing wrong with details or healthy discussions, sometimes the more we complicate something, the more we miss the forest for the trees.

This may be one reason Colton's story has resonated so strongly with so many people. We get to live his journey through his preschool eyes and his pure, childlike faith. He saw what he saw, and because of that, he just wants to tell people that God really, really loves them.

In the video, Sonja mentioned a particular scripture becoming especially vivid to her through Colton's experience. Let's look a little more closely at this passage.

PERSONAL REFLECTION

Read Mark 10:13–16.

Childlike faith—it's not a difficult formula: believing, loving, and following God as His own child, trusting and worshipping as a little one without guile or self-consciousness. Reaching up to our Father and inviting His loving embrace, no matter what our age, is how we experience the kingdom of God today and eternally.

That's not to say that we should not devote ourselves to studying and meditating on Scripture to learn more about God and the ways of faith. We are called to love God with all our hearts, souls, minds, and strength (Mark 12:30). So there is a place for our minds in matters of faith. It is healthy to study and discuss the truths of God's kingdom. But we have limited minds, and hearts that can be deceived. At the end of the day, when it comes to faith, it is comforting to know that we can simply believe God's Word—rely completely on Him and what He's promised, and respond to His love with a childlike faith. When we see a rainbow, we can be reminded that God is the ultimate Promise Keeper. We can trust that heaven is real because our heavenly Father told us so. We can expect God to keep His promises because we can know His character through His revealed Word—the Bible. We can be confident that we can know Him now (Jeremiah 29:13), and that we will know Him even better in heaven (1 Corinthians 13:12). Jesus is with us today (Matthew 18:20), and we will know the ultimate joy of living in our Father's presence throughout eternity (Revelation 21:3).

POINTS TO PONDER

- Why do you think Jesus considered it so important that the children be allowed to come to Him?

- How would you define *childlike faith*?

- How can you balance earnest and serious Bible study with having faith like a child's?

- What is your biggest challenge when it comes to childlike faith? What is your biggest challenge with regard to balancing childlike faith and loving God with all of your mind?

- What steps can you take to begin to overcome those challenges?

- Before this study, did you ever stop and think about rainbows? What will you think of now every time you see a rainbow? What other signs of God's love and faithfulness do you see in the world around you?

- Jesus is God's Son. He came to die in your place and to free you from sin and death. Take time to read John 3:16 and Romans 10:9–13. If you do not know Jesus as your personal Savior, earnestly pray the prayer in the next section. Jesus died for everyone; more important, He died for you.

Journal

Bringing It Home

Read John 14:1–3.

- Jesus referred to heaven as His Father's house. Heaven will be a perfect place. What do you imagine God's house to be like? What will make it perfect?

- Jesus said He is preparing a place for us in His Father's house. Why do you think He's preparing it for us? What do you think Jesus might be doing to prepare for us?

Read Revelation 7:16–17.

- Can you imagine never feeling hungry or thirsty again? Why do you think we won't have those feelings in heaven?

- What things make you sad? How do you think it will feel to never be sad about anything?

- What do you think it means that God will wipe away all tears?

- What do you think "living fountains of water" might be?

- Is heaven a place you want to go when it's time? How do you think you get there?

Read John 3:16 and Romans 10:9–13.

● What do you think these verses mean?

If you want to know Jesus, you may pray the following prayer and be sure that He will hear you and answer. If you choose to pray and you really mean it, Jesus will become your own, personal Savior—He will help you live your life in ways that please God, and one day you can live with Him forever in God's wonderful house.

Prayer for Salvation

Father, I believe. I believe You sent Jesus to die for me and bring me life forever in Your kingdom. Please forgive me for doing wrong things. Help me live my life in ways that please you. I want to be Your child, and I want to live in Your kingdom today and be with You forever. Please accept me into your kingdom and give me new life in You. Jesus, please be Lord of my life and teach me how to be a faithful child of God. Amen.

Family Prayer

Jesus, thank You so much for preparing our home in heaven, Your Father's house. Thank You for loving us enough to return for us and take us to the home You are preparing for us. Until that time, please help us live our best for You here on earth. Help us to love You and to tell others about Your love. Lord, we pray that You will give us the right words to help others know You so that they, too, can live in Your Father's house. Amen.

When Does a Person Go to Heaven?

Heaven is the place you go when you die in the Lord, right? That's what I had always believed and accepted; but when Colton experienced heaven, he had not died. This fact confused me at first, until I remembered Paul's words about a "man in Christ" who was "caught up into Paradise" (2 Corinthians 12:2–4 NKJV).

In the time since Colton's return to us, I have often pondered his experience and marveled at the reality of heaven. To realize it exists *now*, in another realm, to recognize fully that it is a literal place, is the source of such hope and encouragement for our family, as well as those who have shared our experience through our book.

Colton makes no secret of his desire to return. But between now and the time he makes his repeat journey, there is a lot of life for him, and us, to live. Although we intend to live our lives for the Lord and do all He would ask of us here, we all feel a magnetic drawing toward our eternal home. It's hard to imagine anyone would not desire to live in the kingdom of God—to be in His presence and experience the joy only His kingdom can bring.

Though we desire heaven, the reality is that God's kingdom is available to us today. You see, His kingdom is a matter of "now" as well as "not yet." We will one day be transported to God's kingdom that is "not of this world" (John 18:36). But at the same time, we who know Jesus as Savior and Lord experience God's kingdom here on earth because Christ rules our lives, fills our hearts, and operates in power through us. Jesus said that the "kingdom of God is within you" (Luke 17:21). He did not mean that within ourselves we hold some divine quality, but Jesus Himself has taken up residence in the hearts of those who believe (John 17:23). The Spirit of God has been given to us (1 Corinthians 6:19), and we are called to live out the kingdom of God in this world. Romans 14:17 tells us that the "kingdom of God . . . is righteousness, peace and joy in the Holy Spirit."

Jesus taught us to pray, "Your kingdom come, your will be done on earth as it is in heaven" (Matthew 6:10). To enable us to live as children of the kingdom today, doing His will in the world, He sent the Holy Spirit. The Spirit brings: love, joy, peace, longsuffering, kindness, goodness, faithfulness, gentleness, and self-control (Galatians 5:22–23 NKJV). These are qualities of God's own nature at work in our lives. Through them, through us, God's kingdom is here and now. God will use us to point the way for others to know the reality of His eternal kingdom and to share the good news that heaven is for real.

Group Discussion

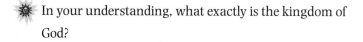 In your understanding, what exactly is the kingdom of God?

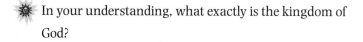 How do Jesus' words "the kingdom of God is within you" make you feel?

✴ Does the kingdom of God live through you? Why or why not?

✴ In your own words, explain the concept that the kingdom of God is both "now" and "not yet."

Watch Session 3
Intro Video Message

In a world that is more concerned with religion than with faith, we are often overtaken by the misconception that we must earn our right to enter heaven. What a dangerous and deeply flawed mind-set! In Psalm 14:2–3, David spoke clearly of our ability to be good enough to purchase our own entry into God's kingdom:

"The LORD looks down from heaven upon the children of men, to see if there are any who understand, who seek God. They have all turned aside, they have together become corrupt; there is none who does good, no, not one" (NKJV).

If we are honest with ourselves, we will own up to the fact that we are incapable of being truly "good." No one knows better than we ourselves just how sinful we can be in our thoughts and attitudes. But God has poured out mercy and grace through His Son. By His death, Jesus made a way for us to receive total forgiveness for sin so we could also obtain righteousness (right standing) in God's sight. Jesus has purchased our freedom with His blood, restored our relationship with our Father, and regained for us our eternal reward. We need only to repent, accept, and believe (Romans 3:21–26).

All of us, even those of us who have accepted Jesus as our Savior, struggle with sinful actions and attitudes (1 John 1:8–9). Just as I did when Colton's life was in danger, we can be overtaken by anger and fear; we may even lash out at God, showing Him disrespect and disdain. But God is not surprised by our actions or words; He is not impressed by our anger, and our fear does not cause Him dismay. God knows exactly what is in our hearts and minds even before we speak; He knows we are incapable of sinless lives (Romans 7:14–25). And God desires that we be honest and transparent before Him. Without honesty before God and willingness to confess our sin, we cannot receive His forgiveness. Without transparency and a readiness to admit our need, we will not receive the abundant life God longs to shower upon us.

Life can teach us to avoid truly disclosing our deepest selves. We fear rejection by others and therefore never allow them to see parts of us that may alienate us from them. But God sees us and knows our hearts before we give them voice, yet He loves us and forgives us in the midst of our ugly reality.

Group Discussion

✷ Has there been a time in your life when you had negative feelings toward God? Share your experience, if you are able.

✷ Read Psalm 139:23–24. What is your reaction? How does being transparent before God make you feel?

✹ Are you confident that you will one day live in God's house—that heaven will be your eternal home? Why or why not?

If at this point you still lack confidence that you will one day live with God in heaven, here's what the Bible tells you to do to be sure: "If you confess with your mouth, 'Jesus is Lord,' and believe in your heart that God raised him from the dead, you will be saved. . . . 'Everyone who calls on the name of the Lord will be saved'" (Romans 10:9, 13).

Do you want to call on Him? If so, pray the prayer for salvation from Session 2.

Watch DVD Session 3

Jesus said, "In the world you will have tribulation; but be of good cheer, I have overcome the world" (John 16:33 NKJV). He did not say we *might* have trouble and sorrow; He said that hard times *will* come. That's because we live on a battleground—all around us a war is being fought between good and evil. We have an enemy who wants to destroy us only because God loves us (1 Peter 5:8). Satan will stop at nothing to try to defeat God's people or keep those who don't know God from finding His love and salvation.

When Colton's condition deteriorated, leaving him lifeless, exhausted, and filled with poison, I was desperate. I was angry at God; at the root of that anger was pure, cold, dreadful fear. I could not accept that my son was dying and I could do nothing to help him. So I called out to God in angry desperation. In utter fear, I raged at Him.

Jesus often told us we should not be afraid (Matthew 10:26, 28, 31; Luke 12:4, 32; Revelation 1:17). When fear overtakes us, it begins to rule our hearts and minds. We become obsessed with the negative "what-ifs" that tomorrow, or the next minute, may hold. Instead of trust, our hearts are filled with dread. Rather than hope, we become mired in hopelessness. When we allow fear to rule, we have ceased to operate in faith. Faith hopes; faith believes; faith trusts in God. Fear denies His love.

Even in my fearful rage, I realized my helplessness. Like the disciples, who, when asked by Jesus if they were going to leave him, answered, "Lord, to whom shall we go? You have the words of eternal life" (John 6:68), I knew that only the Lord could help my son and my family. Only He could restore life, bring comfort, and heal Colton. So I turned to Him in all my ugly humanity. And He heard my prayer!

Sometimes God answers prayers in the way we hope; sometimes He does not. We may not understand the reasons for God's actions or inaction, but we must "walk by faith" even when our lives seem to be falling apart (2 Corinthians 5:7–8 NKJV) and our hearts lay in shreds at our feet. We must come to the place where we can say along with Job, "Though He slay me, yet will I trust Him" (Job 13:15 NKJV).

When our world crumbles beneath us, we can only hold firmly to our Father's love and His promise of eternal life with Him. Though trials and sorrow may be inevitable in this world, we can know the powerful presence of God's kingdom within us today (John 16:33), and in the days to come, we will live with Him in a place where sin cannot enter and Love will always rule.

Scripture

- Isaiah 41:10:

  "Fear not, for I am with you; be not dismayed, for I am your God. I will strengthen you, yes, I will help you, I will uphold you with My righteous right hand." (NKJV)

- Isaiah 43:1–3:

  But now, thus says the Lord, who created you, O Jacob, and He who formed you, O Israel: "Fear not, for I have redeemed you; I have called you by your name; you are Mine. When you pass through the waters, I will be with you; and through the rivers, they shall not overflow you. When you walk through the fire, you shall not be burned, nor shall the flame scorch you. For I am the Lord your God, the Holy One of Israel, your Savior." (NKJV)

- John 16:33:

  "These things I have spoken to you, that in Me you may have peace. In the world you will have tribulation; but be of good cheer, I have overcome the world." (NKJV)

- 2 Timothy 1:7:

  For God has not given us a spirit of fear, but of power and of love and of a sound mind. (NKJV)

- Hebrews 11:1, 6:

  Now faith is the substance of things hoped for, the evidence of things not seen . . . Without faith it is impossible to please [God]. (NKJV)

Group Discussion

※ Have you ever found yourself running from God during difficult times? If so, why, and what was the result?

※ Isaiah 43 says, "*When* you pass through the waters . . ." and "*When* you walk through the fire . . ." It does not say "if." How do you feel knowing life will hold more trials for you?

※ What steps do you believe you can take to face future trials with faith and not fear?

- What place do you believe humility holds in living a life of faith?

- Prayer is an act of faith and humility. What insights can you share about this statement?

- Do you find that you distance yourself from others in times of trial? Do you distance yourself from God? What is the result?

 How can the body of Christ help during difficult times?

 Do you have a story to tell that can encourage the faith of others? Can you share a bit of that now?

 In what ways has this session changed the way you view the kingdom of God?

✳ What thoughts do you now have regarding the kingdom of God being both now and not yet?

✳ Are you assured that heaven will be your eternal home? Why or why not?

Prayer

Father, we praise You for Your limitless love. Thank You for sending Your Son to die for us so we can know life in Your kingdom today and the joy of Your presence for eternity.

Help us learn to live lives of faith and to trust in You even when life holds pain, illness, and loss. Use each of us, Lord, to encourage and strengthen others. Teach us how to live out Your kingdom on earth. Amen.

Real Reflection

It is important to realize that when we face trials, we are not alone. Jesus said, "I am with you always" (Matthew 28:20). And we have the promise of God: "I will never leave you nor forsake you" (Hebrews 13:5 NKJV).

PERSONAL REFLECTION

Read Proverbs 3:5; Psalm 4:4–5; 9:9–10; 18:30–31; 42:5; 62:5–8; 1 John 4:16; 1 Corinthians 2:9; Jeremiah 29:11–12.

My family walked through a year of one trial after another. We asked the same questions and expressed the same frustration that anyone would in those situations. We are not holier or any less human than anyone reading this book. The only foundation on which we could stand during those difficult days was Jesus and our strong belief in His limitless, constant love.

Before we can trust God through the trials that break our hearts and disrupt our lives, we must know that He loves us. Without that absolute knowledge, we cannot trust His plan for our lives when that plan takes us through pain and sorrow.

We are often asked why God chose to answer our prayers and spare Colton's life but has not responded in the same way to similar prayers for others. In answer, I can only say that God is always in control and we can trust Him to only act in ways that are best. God did not send Colton back to us because of any holiness or spiritual superiority on our part; God sent him back because of His love. What is so difficult to understand is that even if God *had* kept Colton in heaven, that, too, would have been an act of love. God cannot operate with any motivation except love because God *is* love. He doesn't *have* love or *give* love; love is the very substance of God's nature.

POINTS TO PONDER

- Do you firmly believe in God's love for you? How does that belief affect the way you face life's trials?

- According to Psalm 56:8, God is so deeply moved when His people suffer that He records their tears. He even saves them! What insight into God's nature does this picture portray?

- Jesus said, "He who has seen me has seen the Father" (John 14:9 NKJV). What attributes were apparent in Jesus when He walked the earth that can enable you to more realistically "see" God?

- Go to your favorite Bible and locate scriptures that give you insight into God's nature. Make a list of the attributes you find.

- In view of all the attributes you have discovered that describe God's nature, what reasons do you have for trusting Him even when life is painful and does not make sense?

Journal

Bringing It Home

- When does a person go to heaven?

- We can live our lives here on earth in ways that show others what heaven will be like. Name some things you can do that will help others understand how wonderful heaven will be.

- What do you think God is like?

- Why should we pray to God?

- Are you ever afraid? How can God help you through those times?

- In the Bible, Jesus said He came to show us what God is like. What are things about Jesus that help you understand God?

- Is it important to trust God even when difficult or sad things happen and you don't understand? Why do you think trusting God is important?

- The Bible says, "God is love" (1 John 4:16). What does that mean to you?

Family Prayer

Father God, we thank You for this time together to learn about You. Help our faith grow, and teach us to trust You at all times. We thank You for Jesus and for the love You have for us. Help us live our lives so others can see how much You love them. Give us the words and the opportunities to tell others about You and the wonderful kingdom of heaven where You live. We want to please You. Help us really understand what that means. Amen.

4

Where Is Heaven?

According to Scripture, Jesus "is seated at the right hand of the throne of the Majesty in the heavens" (Hebrews 8:1 NKJV). Jesus is right where Colton saw Him: in God's throne room, sitting at God's right side. But exactly where is that "throne of the Majesty"? Where is Jesus now, and how do we follow Him? By looking at the changes in Jesus after His resurrection, we may begin to see a picture of what we will experience when we leave the world behind and follow Jesus into our eternal home.

Let's take a look at what we know from God's Word.

After His resurrection, Jesus remained with His disciples for forty days (Acts 1:3). During that time, He appeared to many of His followers. He ate with them, talked with them, and continued to teach them about His Father's kingdom. He also possessed a body that looked much like everyone else's, except it was new; it was different. We know Jesus' appearance must have been a bit altered because Mary Magdalene recognized Him only after He spoke her name; and other followers spent hours with Him before they realized His identity. Apparently, He looked like Himself, yet different. We also know that He did some physically impossible things: He walked through walls (John 20:19, 26), appeared and disappeared at will (Luke 24:31), and defied gravity (Acts 1:9)!

On His last day with His disciples, He promised that He would always be with them and would provide power for them to live out their lives as His witnesses. Then He *rose*—He lifted up into the air and disappeared into the clouds! An angel spoke to His amazed disciples and promised that He would return in the same way (Acts 1:9–11).

So, Jesus rose into the air and was "taken up" into heaven—but exactly where did He go? Where is heaven?

When we consider the location of heaven, we immediately think in terms of direction—heaven is up. It is high above the earth, but exactly how high?

We have discussed the fact that God exists outside of space and time. In that state of being, location is not a relevant concept—it has to do with space. Rather, it may be more appropriate to think of heaven as a world beyond our own. A kingdom or dimension more real, more vibrant, more abundant, more fulfilling than our limited minds can grasp. A higher world, far above our current experience.

In Isaiah 66:1, God tells us, "Heaven is my throne, and the earth is my footstool." We are also told in 1 John 4:16 that "God is love." Love is enthroned in the kingdom of heaven. And that love is given freely to any who will receive. Regardless of heaven's exact location, God loves you and wants you to live there eternally.

Group Discussion

☀ Why do you think Jesus was able to do things that are physically impossible for us?

☀ Jesus rose into the air and disappeared into the clouds. What impact do you believe this may have had on those who witnessed it?

✺ What are the most difficult concepts for you to grasp when you consider the lack of space and time in heaven?

✺ God created heaven to be our eternal home; Jesus invited us to live there with Him forever. What feelings do these facts stir in your heart?

Watch Session 4 Intro Video Message

Monuments, memorials, statues—Washington, D.C., is filled with our country's best attempts to honor our nation's heroes and define our national identity. When we visit our homeland's seat of power, we are surrounded by reminders of the glory that is the United States. We are filled with gratitude, but humbled by the sacrifices given on our behalf. Our nation's capital is grand indeed; however, Washington's greatest efforts at grandeur and glory, while patriotically inspiring, still leave us as hollow as its marble halls. National patriotism gives us a way to live, but does not supply a reason.

Only in relationship with the Creator can we find reason and purpose. Only through the sacrifice of Jesus Christ can we discover the true freedom our hearts long to find.

And only in His presence can we realize our genuine identity, for "in him we live and move and have our being" (Acts 17:28). He is our homeland!

Heaven is the place Jesus prepared for us to celebrate life in Him forever. Monuments and marble halls cannot compare with streets of gold and the throne room of God. Nothing on this earth can compare to the eternal home Jesus has prepared for those who believe!

While we can easily find Washington, D.C., with a road map or a GPS, no GPS on this earth can give us the coordinates for heaven. But Jesus said that those who belong to Him already know the way. In fact, He went on to say, "I am the way" (John 14:4–6). Jesus came to lead us to our heavenly Father and to enable us to experience eternal life with Him in His kingdom.

But where is God's kingdom? Often in the Old Testament, especially in Psalms, we are told that God is our dwelling place

(Psalm 90:1; 91:9). Precisely where He is located or in what dimension, we cannot know. However, we know that we are "in Him," that we actually abide in Him, and that He is love (1 John 4:16). Whatever the exact locale of heaven, we know it exists in the center of God's love.

Group Discussion

※ Have you ever visited a monument or memorial that impacted you? In what way?

※ How did the actual experience measure up to your expectations?

❁ Do you ever experience anticipation of your eventual experience of heaven? How so?

❁ Heaven is more an experience than a place. Do you agree with that statement? What does that statement mean to you?

❁ What did Jesus mean when He said, "I am the way" (John 14:6)?

Watch DVD Session 4

Often in Scripture (NKJV), the things of God are referred to as being "above" (Colossians 3:1; Psalm 50:4, 144:7; Romans 10:6). Whether or not we are to understand "above" as an elevated, spatial location, we can only speculate. Not even Colton can say exactly where he was when he was in heaven. But he can tell you that an angel carried him up past the clouds.

So many aspects of Colton's journey make us ask along with Mary, "How can this be?" We can only echo Gabriel's response, "With God nothing [is] impossible" (Luke 1:34, 37 NKJV). So many details about eternity are unclear to us in this world. But one day, we will know even as we are known, and all our questions will be answered (1 Corinthians 13:12). For now, we can only glean the truth as it is presented to us in God's Word—the Bible.

For our family, Colton's experience created many questions. We turned to Scripture—our final authority—for answers and guidance. Following are some issues we encountered and the scriptural truths we discovered.

WINGS

There are many scriptural references to a variety of creatures in heaven, including people, that had *wings*. Here are some examples:

Then I looked up—and there before me were two women, with
the wind in their wings! They had wings like those of a stork.
(Zech. 5:9)

Hide me in the shadow of your wings. (Psalm 17:8)

How precious is Your lovingkindness, O God! Therefore the
children of men put their trust under the shadow of Your wings.
(Psalm 36:7 NKJV)

The four living creatures, each having six wings, were full of
eyes around and within. And they do not rest day or night,
saying: "Holy, holy, holy, Lord God Almighty, Who was and is and
is to come!" (Revelation 4:8 NKJV)

Colton says we will all be given wings in heaven. Even
though this seems like an incredible upgrade, the Bible doesn't
mention this as fact. But there is no scripture that clearly
objects either. The Bible is silent on this issue.

HEAVENLY BODIES

Colton saw only young people in heaven: his great-grandfather
(who died at age sixty-one, many years before Colton was
born) was a young man, without the glasses he wore on earth.
However, Colton's unborn, older sister seemed to be aging at
a normal "earthly" rate. Age is really a moot point in heaven
because heaven exists outside of space and time. Our heavenly
"age" will be the perfect one, as *all* things will be perfect in

heaven. According to Scripture, all earthly imperfections and infirmities will cease once we enter our eternal home.

> And I heard a loud voice from heaven saying, "Behold, the tabernacle of God is with men, and He will dwell with them, and they shall be His people. God Himself will be with them and be their God. And God will wipe away every tear from their eyes; there shall be no more death, nor sorrow, nor crying. There shall be no more pain, for the former things have passed away." Then He who sat on the throne said, "Behold, I make all things new." And He said to me, "Write, for these words are true and faithful." (Revelation 21:3–5 NKJV)

> So also is the resurrection of the dead. The body is sown in corruption, it is raised in incorruption. It is sown in dishonor, it is raised in glory. It is sown in weakness, it is raised in power. It is sown a natural body, it is raised a spiritual body. There is a natural body, and there is a spiritual body. . . . And the dead will be raised incorruptible, and we shall be changed. For this corruptible must put on incorruption, and this mortal must put on immortality. (1 Corinthians 15:42–44, 52–53 NKJV)

> Beloved, now we are children of God; and it has not yet been revealed what we shall be, but we know that when He is revealed, we shall be like Him, for we shall see Him as He is. (1 John 3:2 NKJV)

HEAVENLY "TIME"

We have discussed a bit about the absence of space and time in heaven. It's a concept so alien to our experience that it's hard to grasp, let alone communicate. Colton says he was in heaven for "three minutes," yet he experienced what could have taken weeks on earth. We also know that in heaven there is no sun or moon; God is the light there. There is nothing to mark time because time is not.

> But, beloved, do not forget this one thing, that with the Lord one day is as a thousand years, and a thousand years as one day. (2 Peter 3:8 NKJV)

> For a thousand years in Your sight are like yesterday when it is past. (Psalm 90:4 NKJV)

> The city had no need of the sun or of the moon to shine in it, for the glory of God illuminated it. The Lamb is its light. (Revelation 21:23 NKJV)

> There shall be no night there: They need no lamp nor light of the sun, for the Lord God gives them light. (Revelation 22:5 NKJV)

> Read Genesis 1.

MARKERS

For our family, Colton's experience has raised many questions. One of these concerns is what Colton called "markers" in Jesus' hands and feet. Some historians claim it was the Roman practice in crucifixion to drive nails through the victims' wrists rather than the palms of the hands. The account in the gospel of John supports Colton's observation of pierced hands rather than pierced wrists.

> After he said this, he showed them his hands and side. The disciples were overjoyed when they saw the Lord. (John 20:20)
>
> Now Thomas (called Didymus), one of the Twelve, was not with the disciples when Jesus came. So the other disciples told him, "We have seen the Lord!"
> But he said to them, "Unless I see the nail marks in his hands and put my finger where the nails were, and put my hand into his side, I will not believe."
> A week later his disciples were in the house again, and Thomas was with them. Though the doors were locked, Jesus came and stood among them and said, "Peace be with you!" Then he said to Thomas, "Put your finger here; see my hands. Reach out your hand and put it into my side. Stop doubting and believe." (John 20:24–27)

Those who have studied death by crucifixion say one common cause of death was asphyxiation. The reason the Jewish leaders asked for Jesus' legs to be broken was to hasten death by making it impossible for him to support himself by pushing up with his feet for air. This would indicate that the majority of Jesus' body weight was supported by his feet, not by his hands. In this case, nails would not have torn through Jesus' hands.

Now it was the day of Preparation, and the next day was to be
a special Sabbath. Because the Jewish leaders did not want the
bodies left on the crosses during the Sabbath, they asked Pilate
to have the legs broken and the bodies taken down. The soldiers
therefore came and broke the legs of the first man who had been
crucified with Jesus, and then those of the other. But when they
came to Jesus and found that he was already dead, they did not
break his legs. (John 19:31–32)

Group Discussion

⁕ Why do you think God's kingdom (heaven) is beyond our
total comprehension?

⁕ According to 1 Corinthians 13:12, we now see as through
a dim "mirror." What do you believe that means?

✹ How does it make you feel knowing that you will one day know even as you are known by God? What do you think that means?

✹ What do you think of having wings in heaven?

✹ How do you believe a spiritual body differs from a "natural" or physical body?

✴ What do you think it means to "put on immortality" (1 Corinthians 15:53 NKJV)?

✴ How does the fact that God created the sun and moon give insight into time in God's kingdom?

✴ First John 1:5 says that "God is light." What are your thoughts on that?

✸ Second Peter 3:8 says, "With the Lord one day is as a thousand years, and a thousand years as one day" (NKJV). What do you believe that means?

Prayer

Father God, on this day, we cannot know You fully; but one day, we will. We know we cannot grasp the majesty and mystery of Your kingdom, but please reveal to us all we need to know for today. Thank You for making us Your children and for preparing a place for us to live with you forever. In Jesus' name we pray. Amen.

Real Reflection

We read in 1 Corinthians 13:12 that one day, in heaven, we will know as we are known. We will know because we will see. We will see God and His eternal kingdom. Colton saw these things and has encouraged us all with his experiences. He saw wings; he saw lights surrounding people; he saw vibrant people in their primes; he saw angels; he saw past, present, and future. But the thing that most impressed Colton was the overwhelming love of God. God's love is so big that it was a part of Colton's every experience in heaven. Colton was known and Colton knew—He knew God's love. Now He encourages everyone to know the overwhelming power of that love.

PERSONAL REFLECTION

Read Ephesians 3:17–19.

While we are living in the "now" of God's kingdom, our knowledge is limited. But though we are incomplete in our comprehension of the things of God, there are things we can know and experience. Heaven is the fulfillment of God's kingdom, but we do not have to wait for heaven to experience the power of God's love.

In Ephesians 3, Paul prays that his fellow followers of Jesus Christ will be able to comprehend the full measure of God's love.

He says that all followers of Christ (saints) can comprehend this love and that this understanding can actually go beyond mere knowledge. It is a matter of heart and spirit, not just of mind and intellect. We can know all about someone without ever having spent any time with that individual. We can know his or her name, background, and the things that person has done or said. But without a personal relationship, we really don't fully *know* that person. Comprehending the true width and length and depth and height of God's love is much the same way. Without experiencing a personal relationship with God, without engaging our hearts as well as our minds, we cannot truly know Him or fully know His love.

While the full experience of heaven will be far beyond anything we can imagine, we are not left to wait without any consolation. Instead, we can already begin to know God and to live in His kingdom. We can read His Word and spend time in prayer and conversation with Him. We can get to know Him personally; and through that, we can begin to comprehend His love on all the levels of understanding we possess. While we do see dimly now, we can still see. We can still experience God's love. As Paul told us in Ephesians, when Christ dwells in our hearts and we are rooted in love, we can begin to perceive how huge God's love is. We start to appreciate the profound truth in Colton's simple statement: "God loves us so much, so much."

POINTS TO PONDER

- Why do you think that, out of everything Colton experienced, he always comes back to talking about how much God loves us?

- We know that God's kingdom is both "now" and "not yet." How do 1 Corinthians 13:12 and Ephesians 3:17–19 help us understand this concept?

- Who is your favorite actor? Who is your best friend? What are the differences in your knowledge of these two people? With this in mind, what does it mean to know God?

- Why do you believe God chose to let us experience part of His kingdom here on earth while we await its total fulfillment in heaven?

- Have you experienced God's love personally? If not, what steps can you take to discover its reality for yourself?

Journal

Bringing It Home

- Where do *you* think heaven is?

- Jesus is sitting right beside God in heaven. What do you think He's doing there?

- Jesus died on the cross for you. That is a wonderful thing. But He also rose from the dead—He came back to life! When He did, He looked pretty much the same as before, but He could do marvelous, amazing things: walk through walls, disappear suddenly, and rise up into the air. Why do you think Jesus could do these things?

- We know heaven exists, but we can't see it until God allows us to. Colton went to heaven, but he didn't die. Why do you think God showed him heaven while he was still alive?

- Colton said that he could fly in heaven. Do you believe people in heaven can fly? If so, why do you think they do? What do you think that will be like for you?

- Colton wants to ask God why there are bugs on earth. What would you like to ask God?

- The Bible says, "God is light" (1 John 1:5). What do you think that means?

- "With God nothing [is] impossible" (Luke 1:37 NKJV). What kinds of things can God do?

- Do you know that God says we can actually know Him? He says all we have to do is really want to and ask Him and He will help us understand what He is like. What are some things you know about God now?

Family Prayer

Father, we thank You again for Your love and for creating heaven for us. It will be so wonderful when we live there with You. But until that day, please help us to live lives that are pleasing to You. Help us to love others and to help them see how amazing You are. Thank You for our family and for letting us all be part of Your family here on Earth and in heaven. We want to learn more about You every day. Thank You for teaching us about how big Your love is. Amen.

Who Goes to Heaven?

One evening, while Jesus walked the earth as a man, Nicodemus, a Pharisee, came to speak with Him. Nicodemus believed Jesus had come from God and recognized the power of God in His life. But what Jesus said to him was shocking: "Most assuredly, I say to you, unless one is born again, he cannot see the kingdom of God" (John 3:3 NKJV).

Nicodemus was confused. "How can a man be born when he is old?" he asked. "Can he enter a second time into his mother's womb and be born?" (v. 4 NKJV).

Nicodemus did not realize Jesus was speaking of a spiritual event, not a natural one.

Just as we are physically born into *this* world, we must be spiritually born into God's kingdom. By receiving this new spiritual life, we enter into a new realm; it is a new state of being in which we discover the "now" of God's kingdom and gain assurance of the "not yet." In the "now" we are saved from the penalty of sin and death by accepting Jesus' death on our behalf. And though it is "not yet," we are assured of eternal life in God's kingdom to come—heaven—where we will live in God's perfect presence through eternity.

But how does this new birth take place?

We learned earlier that Jesus said, "I am the way and the truth and the life" (John 14:6). Jesus is the way we find this new life—through Him we experience spiritual birth into the kingdom of God. In Romans 10:9, we learn that "if you confess with your mouth the Lord Jesus and believe in your heart that God has raised Him from the dead, you will be saved" (NKJV). Simply stated, if you believe that Jesus is the Son of God and that He died for your sins and rose again in victory over death, new life in Him is yours for the asking.

Who goes to heaven? Those who "confess" and "believe" in Jesus and the salvation available to all who will receive new life in Him.

You may ask about Colton's sister or other children who have not had opportunity to know and receive salvation through Jesus. How can they enter heaven? Salvation is needed only where sin exists. A child too young to know right from wrong cannot truly choose to sin. Jesus said, "Let the little children come to Me, and do not forbid them; for of such is the kingdom of God" (Luke 18:16). No doubt, that is why Colton said repeatedly, "Jesus really, really loves the children."

Group Discussion

Can you relate to Nicodemus? In what way?

Have you experienced the spiritual birth discussed in this session? If so, share a bit of your experience. If not, do you have any questions you would like answered?

✻ Have you ever confessed to others your personal relationship with Jesus? Was it difficult? Why or why not?

✻ Those who know Jesus as their Savior will one day live with Him and with God in heaven. Does this promise bring you comfort? In what way?

Watch Session 5
Intro Video Message

Many of us have experienced the loss of a loved one. We know the pain of separation and the sorrow of saying good-bye. Death can cause us fear and great heartache; it seems an irrevocable end. However, Colton's experience plays out in vivid reality the fact that for those who know Christ, death is not an end, but a beginning. Rather than seeking closure of lost relationships, we need to seek patience, for one day, we will be reunited with those we love in the kingdom of God.

Colton expresses his desire to return to heaven. His feelings must be much like Paul's. The apostle found it difficult to choose between life in Christ's service here and eternal life in heaven (Philippians 1:22–24). He said that to "live is Christ and to die is gain" (v. 21). Paul realized, as Colton does, that heaven is an amazing place of perfection, where we will be reunited with those who have gone before, but more important, we will be united with God.

First Thessalonians 4:13 says we do not grieve as those who have no hope, but rest in a certain hope of reunion—not only with God, but with those we love. Those who possess this hope have Christ's promise, "Peace I leave with you, My peace I give to you; not as the world gives do I give to you. Let not your heart be troubled, neither let it be afraid" (John 14:27 NKJV). Finding closure when we lose a loved one to physical death may bring a measure of peace, but that poor substitute cannot compare to the perfect peace that can be ours through faith in Jesus.

Group Discussion

✻ Have you ever experienced the seeming hopelessness of losing someone you love? What other feelings did you have?

✻ What got you through that time? Did you ever receive true peace? How?

✺ What are your feelings about death?

✺ Do you truly see heaven as your home? If so, in what way? If not, why?

✺ In what ways can you relate to Paul's conflict—whether to remain here or go on to be with Jesus?

Watch DVD Session 5

By now, we hope you have come to understand that physical death is really a passage into life for those who know Jesus. We don't die and *leave* home; we pass from life to life and *go* home.

Here on earth, our temporary home, our lives become overtaken by cares. Our focus is often determined by each day's concerns and challenges. Even for those of us who know the salvation of Jesus, our focus can be divided and clouded by the distractions of life. We see "in a mirror, dimly" (1 Corinthians 13:12 NKJV). It can seem as though this world is the only true reality. But since Colton returned to us with his report of heaven, that spiritual kingdom is now the one that gains our concentration and defines true reality for our family.

Although we still get distracted by the circumstances of life, we now have a constant reminder that this world is only for a time. We need to keep our eyes focused on God's kingdom and cling to His promise rather than allow the cares of this life to weigh us down and defeat us. We now try to always keep those things of eternal significance before our eyes and alive in our hearts.

One of the most powerful things Colton has told us about heaven is that "the first person you will see is Jesus." Imagine! What is it like to look into the eyes that beheld creation before it was complete? What is it like to see the smile that can light a kingdom? To feel the embrace of the arms that stretched wide on the cross to save us? To feel the touch of the hands that were pierced? To hear the voice that echoes through eternity, "Come, you blessed of My Father, inherit the kingdom prepared for you from the foundation of the world" (Matthew 25:34 NKJV)?

What a glorious way to step into eternity!

Scripture

- Philippians 3:12–14:

  Not that I have already attained, or am already perfected; but I press on, that I may lay hold of that for which Christ Jesus has also laid hold of me. Brethren, I do not count myself to have apprehended; but one thing I do, forgetting those things which are behind and reaching forward to those things which are ahead, I press toward the goal for the prize of the upward call of God in Christ Jesus. (NKJV)

- Hebrews 12:1–2:

  Therefore we also, since we are surrounded by so great a cloud of witnesses, let us lay aside every weight, and the sin which so easily ensnares us, and let us run with endurance the race that is set before us, looking unto Jesus, the author and finisher of our faith, who for the joy that was set before

Him endured the cross, despising the shame, and has sat down at the right hand of the throne of God. (NKJV)

● Matthew 6:25–34:

"Therefore I say to you, do not worry about your life, what you will eat or what you will drink; nor about your body, what you will put on. Is not life more than food and the body more than clothing? Look at the birds of the air, for they neither sow nor reap nor gather into barns; yet your heavenly Father feeds them. Are you not of more value than they? Which of you by worrying can add one cubit to his stature? So why do you worry about clothing? Consider the lilies of the field, how they grow: they neither toil nor spin; and yet I say to you that even Solomon in all his glory was not arrayed like one of these. Now if God so clothes the grass of the field, which today is, and tomorrow is thrown into the oven, will He not much more clothe you, O you of little faith? Therefore do not worry, saying, 'What shall we eat?' or 'What shall we drink?' or 'What shall we wear?' For after all these things the Gentiles seek. For your heavenly Father knows that you need all these things. But seek first the kingdom of God and His righteousness, and all these things shall be added to you. Therefore do not worry about tomorrow, for tomorrow will worry about its own things. Sufficient for the day is its own trouble." (NKJV)

Group Discussion

What are your thoughts regarding the fact that we don't *leave* home when we die in the Lord, but we *go* home?

What are some distractions in your life that cause you to lose focus on the fact that heaven is the true reality?

❋ What steps can you take in your own life to guard against being distracted by the cares of this world?

❋ What do you think your feelings will be when you first see Jesus with your own eyes?

❋ What do you think His first words to you will be?

What do you see when you look at the drawing of Jesus in the book?

Has this study caused you to feel more compelled to share your faith with others? In what way?

Colton was able to see the past, the present, and the future from heaven. With this in mind, what do you believe the writer of Hebrews meant by the statement "We are surrounded by so great a cloud of witnesses" (12:1 NKJV)?

☀ What do you think "Seek first the kingdom of God" means? (See Matthew 6:33 NKJV.) How can you practice that in your own life?

Prayer

Father, You are so worthy of all our praise. Nothing we have to give can express our gratitude. You created us; You loved us in spite of our sinful selves; You saved us; You prepared an eternal paradise for us—You desire to have us with you for eternity! You are the Creator of the universe; nothing exists without You, yet You love sinful humanity with an intensity we cannot comprehend. Thank You for making the way for us to have a relationship with You. Amen.

Real Reflection

Jesus wanted us to understand God's kingdom. However, the things of God are so far beyond our world that it can be difficult to grasp them. That's why Jesus taught in parables (stories about common things that explain or define the uncommon)—to help us understand things about God and His kingdom.

Jesus spoke often about heaven. He wanted to remind us that this world is not our home. He wanted us to look beyond the trials and pain we might find in this world and keep our eyes on the things that have eternal significance. Not that Jesus does not understand the pain we experience in this world; as a matter of fact, in Psalm 56:8, we read that God actually records our pain and cherishes our tears. He cries them with us.

PERSONAL REFLECTION

Read Matthew 13:1–9, 18–23, 44–46.

POINTS TO PONDER

- What painful life experiences have come to mind during this last session? What were your feelings toward God during those sorrowful times? What are your feelings now?

- As you read Matthew 13:1–9, which type of soil best describes you? Why?

- What is the hidden treasure spoken of in Matthew 13:44? Do you own this treasure? Explain.

- In what way is heaven like a "pearl of great price" (v. 46 NKJV)?

- What have you learned in this study that has been life changing? How do you now view heaven?

- What aspects of heaven, as Colton experienced it and as Scripture has presented it, have most captivated you? Why?

Journal

Bringing It Home

- Who goes to heaven? Why do you think this is true?

- Now that we've reached the end of our study, do you know how you can be sure that you will live with Jesus in God's house (heaven)?

- Jesus said, "Let the little children come to Me, and do not forbid them; for of such is the kingdom of God" (Luke 18:16 NKJV). When Colton came back from heaven, he kept telling everyone, "Jesus really, really loves the children." Why do you think Jesus loves kids so much?

- What do you think "peace" means?

- The Bible tells us that Jesus will give us peace that is deeper than we can ever understand, even when we lose something or someone we love. What do you think that kind of peace feels like?

- Heaven is "perfect." Having completed this study, do you understand what that statement really means?

- What does the word *death* mean to you? Does that frighten you? (Parents, if your children are also participating in this study, please consider each child's maturity level before allowing him or her to watch this session's DVD with you.)

- Why should Colton's time in heaven help us not be afraid of death?

- What about heaven are you most looking forward to?

- What do you think it will be like to see Jesus?

- Do you think He will know you? Will you know Him?

Family Prayer

Father God, life can be so wonderful, but sometimes it's really hard. We thank You for the good times and ask You to help us with the hard ones. Help us always remember that You created a place for us to live with You where there will be no more hard times. We want to help others know all about You and what it's like in heaven. Please give us the courage to tell others about You and Your amazing love. Amen.

Conclusion

Taken from Revelation 22 (NKJV)

And he showed me a pure river of water of life, clear as crystal, proceeding from the throne of God and of the Lamb. In the middle of its street, and on either side of the river, was the tree of life, which bore twelve fruits, each tree yielding its fruit every month. The leaves of the tree were for the healing of the nations. And there shall be no more curse, but the throne of God and of the Lamb shall be in it, and His servants shall serve Him. They shall see His face, and His name shall be on their foreheads. There shall be no night there: They need no lamp nor light of the sun, for the Lord God gives them light. And they shall reign forever and ever.

Then he said to me . . . "Behold, I am coming quickly, and My reward is with Me, to give to every one according to his work. I am the Alpha and the Omega, the Beginning and the End, the First and the Last." . . . And the Spirit and the bride say, "Come!" And let him who hears say, "Come!" And let him who thirsts come. Whoever desires, let him take the water of life freely . . . He who testifies to these things says, "Surely I am coming quickly." Amen. Even so, come, Lord Jesus! The grace of our Lord Jesus Christ be with you all. Amen.

Share the same comfort and assurance you received from *Heaven is for Real* with your children!

Uniquely written from a child for a child, *Heaven is for Real for Kids* is Colton Burpo's telling of his trip to Heaven. Colton shares a very important message that will speak to every child's heart... **"Jesus really, really loves the children!"**

Beautifully illustrated, the book also includes a Question and Answer section helping kids understand what the Bible says about heaven.

More information at www.heavenisforreal.net

**AVAILABLE
NOVEMBER 2011**

Read the complete story of Colton's trip to heaven and back in this #1 *New York Times* best-selling book by his dad.

Also available as a special Deluxe Edition. Complete with color photos and a presentation page, this treasured keepsake is perfect for gift-giving.

THOMAS NELSON
Since 1798

thomasnelson.com

eReader™
version
available